AF436849

- Belgio -

THE ART
OF THE WORD

SHAPES IN THE MIST

◆

Translated by
Antonello Di Carlo
DC TRADUZIONI

EDIZIONI WE

00belgio@gmail.com

ISBN: 979-12-5497-062-1
©2022 Edizioni WE di Nicola Bergamaschi
Via Paulli 10/A - 26015 -Soresina (CR)
www.clickpertutti.com
www.edizioniwe.com
www.facebook.com/edizioniwe
www.instagram.com/edizioniwe
info@edizioniwe.com

INTRODUCTION

Life often puts obstacles in front of us, that initially appear insurmountable to the eye.

Our growth and future depend on our determination to overcome them.

I believe in love and happiness, in a world where there is a precise balance in every detail.

Hatred and repression are opposed by love and freedom. We are all fruits of our past, our sufferings and even our mistakes, we are all called to an existence dedicated to our fellow,man, in the hope that he will come first and dedicate himself to us.

The most important source in the world is the word, we are perpetually conditioned by the words,emotions and feelings are provoked by them, but in the end,the word is a choice, it is we who decide whether to say "I love you" or "I hate you", so why don't we all work together for a happier and more cohesive world? Wouldn't that be easier? Why do we have to be slaves to envy and animalistic ignorance? No one in the world is... It shows itself to be so, but it is not.

Don't be afraid of words, say a few more "I love you",
give a few more hugs. One day,all these "small" gestu-
res could be mothers of regrets. Be happy, be human
lovers of the world, be a family,even with those who
do not share your blood.

Matteo Belgiovane

THE ART OF THE WORD

SHAPES IN THE MIST

ROCK

So much time spent there,
thinking while I was there,
observing the horizon,
lost among the silences and voids,
interrupted by the waves of the sea.
I will never forget
where I come from
I will never forget
what I hold in my heart
I was lost between a glass
of beer in the monotony
Then, you came into my poetry changing
every rhyme and pattern.
The sadness, slowly,faded away
The winter that passed the sun,
that rose the spring,that was almost here.
I wrote entire texts against love,
thinking it was only the consequence
of a mutual need.
It comes from nothing,
even from a glance,
that's what love is all about,
valuing every little gesture
and ignoring all the rest.

WITHOUT NAME*

I look at myself in the mirror:
my face is aged,
my ribs look like waves on my skin,
the swollen eyes full of pain.
Man kills when is full
of fear and devoid of colour.
The moans of my roommates grew louder
All huddled together,
sleeping next to the dead.
An acrid, almost suffocating smell,
the writing on the walls of farewells,
carved with nails.
I wondered where God was.
Death was assailing me,
slowly I was giving up,
my last thought was of my daughter,
who would raise my family tomorrow.
And the chimney was smoking,
my soul was flying.
I and all the other victims of hatred,
the man blinded by a murderous fury,
ready to spill blood,
soiling the white snow that had,
innocently, settled on the ground.
I did not die, I was only reborn
in a world without anger
and unfounded prejudices.

** Written after a visit to the San Sabba concentration camp (Trieste)*

FEAR

The lights of the villages
decorate the mountains,
like stars in the sky,
indicating the right course.
A lighthouse flashes,as
the fog obliterates
the surrounding landscape.
The sea seems to isolate
this remote island.
We are all victims
of a two-tone world,
almost as if it takes away
our three-dimensional view,
giving a homogeneity
to our characters,
making us all useless:
photocopies destined
to continuous suffering
and repression,
in a world that crushes us,
like plastic bottles.
In the thickest fog,
look up and search the sky
for a star that can orient you.
Put your hands forward
and anticipate the obstacles.

LAMPS

It was an evening like any other,
where the concern was the art test.
Immersed in the dreams of all nights,
mother was sleeping peacefully.
But,suddenly, time stopped,
the earth, suddenly, trembled,
frightened mother took me in her arms
and took me outside with a thousand others.
The clock stopped at a quarter past three,
as if everything had turned off,
the town was falling to the ground
after thousands of years.
My mother didn't know what to say.
Dad was digging with others,
searching for a voice.
We lost everything,
even memories, but after all,
the past cannot be erased.
We will start again from the rubble
for a life without misery,
where you observe
the stars on top of the mountain,
where you truly appreciate yourself.

LIVING

If you think you don't shine
enough in your life,
think of the moon,
which, in its insignificant size in space,
has the power to illuminate
our inspiring nights.
Writers, poets and painters....
If you stop believing in yourself,
think of the waves
that,even though they always
find the rock to stop their race,
 always have the strength to try again.
Never give up at the first obstacle
This is what the sea teaches us.
If you feel useless,
think of the constellations:
each star is a very important point.
If you get lost,
look for the reason within yourself.
It will bring you back
to port, like a lighthouse.
Be a family,
because family is fuel
for the wonderful machine of life!
Be happy!
Otherwise, your days will seem
insuperable and colourless.

Be sad at times!
That's a good thing, too.
Remember that there is
no spring without winter.
Be strong!

PACIFIC

People who threaten themselves,
a few who put their faces on.
Some people scar it with acid.
The heart in some people
is really greedy:
mothers who kill their children,
fathers killing mothers,
faces of broken families,
painted in pictures.
Nobody thinks about themselves.
A depressed person who makes
an extreme gesture...
In France, they know a lot about violence
They shoot in a theatre full of talent
In London, the Thames flows,
people are running,
the world declines.
Hate is our undoing:
people hanging themselves,
because in the world they don't stand out.
Nations shooting missiles
at each other,from one
end of the world to the other.
Meanwhile, the planet
goes round and round again,
from the North Pole
to the South Pole:the ice is gone,

you can no longer breathe
with nuclear power.
A flower in Syria,
a flower in all of Africa.
There has been no peace
for about a thousand years.
Waiting for the crisis to end,
in America,the protest begins.
In Europe, terror wears a shirt
Italy dreams of an idealistic future
New reasons are taken to the streets
Those who cry welcome them
Some say: "Let's sink them!"
The fact is that Children die
and God takes note.
In short, people
who threaten themselves,
a few who put their faces on.
Where is the brain?
We'll certainly start again,
but we don't know when.
They say the Middle Ages
has already passed,
but meanwhile,children
are playing with guns.

HORIZON

On the seashore,
she looked at the horizon,
while her husband
and his ship were turning.
The wind blows hard
from bow to stern
He blames his life on it.
The fast boat disappeared,
An "I love you" shouted
No one heard it.
A tear tears the heart
She misses him,
she wants him back.
Six months without him....
the soul dies.
Diana looks at the sea,
the fog obscures infinity,
love hinders freedom.
On the balcony, she waits with a smile...
the habit of having a wounded heart.
The village of fishermen
stood silently watching,
as the woman stood there,waiting.
The stars covered by clouds
made the nights darker
From the sea, no light
had been seen for months

A young son he left behind
 Pregnant Diana waited every night
The night and the rain covered the sobs,
punctual as the minutes and chimes.

IMPERVIOUS

A tear falls from the sky,
fast and uncontested.
The betrayed, but first,
faithful honesty,is forever
proclaimed by my sword.
I consider myself worthy
of an enlightened paradise
I grew meek in historical darkness.
The icy cold is felt by the skin,
followed by shivers
and heaviness of my breath.
The bigger a candle is,
the easier it is to break,
but a small candle
however strong it is,
its flame will shine
for much less time.
I,who sell memories, as
if they were money,
in front of emptiness,
I am frightened,
falling into an unbecoming
state to my person,
losing my theme and verb to live.
No matter how hard a human tries,
his life will be a succession
of flowers and brambles,

because there is no descent,
without first having made an ascent,
because there is no plain,
without the existence of mountains.

PSYCHE

And my heart burns
The soul saturated
with energy,
vanishes in nothingness.
Where the death
of summer rises,
the cold is born.
But looking deeply
into my heart,
I feel warmth
and an immense feeling
of love.
The same one that,
closing my eyes,
lights my way to new regions.
The alternation
of the driving rain
and the baking sun dries up
the surrounding nature.
I wander helplessly
and alone, lost, looking
at the firmament,
searching for the north,
deceived by the multitude
of false stars,
which like negative
thoughts to confuse my soul.

I seek immensity in cosmic nothingness
I seek a rose in the desert,
because where there is nothing,
every smallness becomes abundance.
He, who has fed only
with bitterness in life,
will know how to taste
the sweet of a good palace.

THE INCONSCIO

Like water in a torrent,
time flows.
I stop to hear
my boundless silences,
losing reason
and intellect in the void,
giving a sweet breath
to the demons,
who, in voracious sadness,
also, dark and colourless, feed.
Slowly, as hope fades,
even the last smile disappears.
And I,cowardly,pretend!
Humiliating my person
and my goals,
shipwrecked in the sea,
without ever launching an SOS,
because of a proud sailor,
trying to be a hero.
And the water presses down on me,
depriving me of breath,
leaving me to ponder about
who knows what question,
posed by an unfounded idea.
People, watch
and enjoy every moment!
Do not forget that

every gesture has meaning,
every action has a consequence,
every unit of time has value.

QUIET

Hermione,all is silent!
The wind caresses
your hair and the clouds
cover your head, like an umbrella.
Maiden Hermione,
of candid soul,
you stand in contrast
to the darkness
of this dreary season.
The years pass,
but you do not grow old.
Your bright eyes light up
when you meet my eyes,
like planets that do not shine
with their own light.
Oh,Hermione, all is silent!
Listen to yourself!
Speak to yourself,Hermione!
Love yourself and love me!
Smile, Hermione!Sing
together with the forest.
Hermione,live! Don't turn
your life into a forced cohabitation!

MINUTES AND CHIMES

The rain falls on the roof
of the car and you think,
you stare at the void
and,of course, you breathe.
But you lose yourself
in that deafening sound,
that actually causes so much silence,
an unbearable deep silence.
The hands are like runners race
on the pendulum.
Tick tock, tick tock... each chime
will not be returned to you.
Let us enjoy life!
Let us lose ourselves in it,
because it is when you lose yourself,
that you truly find your way.
When you get lost,you stare
carefully at each point,
giving it its rightful place.
There are millions of stars
in the sky,
but only one points north.
Just stare at it and let it guide you
in the right direction.
Remember that the days will change,
the hours will change,
the minutes and seconds will change,

the year will change,
moods and even seasons will change,
but only one thing will never change...
the soul.

TO YOU

The passing of time
escapes my gaze
In your eyes, I was looking
at the firmament,
it is so deep and mysterious.
But it's easy for me
to find my way
in that multitude of stars.
Quickly,a deep happiness
appeared to me,
that, like fire,
still burns in my heart.
Bigger and stronger
the flame ever appears.
The wind gently caresses
your face,
as my hands graze your features.
We'll face life united,
without ever giving up,
because love can be deprived
of everything... even of time,
but with feeling, it is
always sweet and strong.

GROW

They say that life
is a collection of colours:
green, red, orange,
yellow, blue and many more.
But over time, they tend to fade:
from warm, cold, primary
or secondary colours to neutral ones.
Over time, stars tend not to be
observed with the fine eye of a child,
but begin to be scrutinised
with more geometry,
as if in time, everything
must follow some stupid logic.
A child smiles even
at a stylised sheep.
Do you know those drawings
you can't understand?
An adult looks at them,
smiles, and then,puts them aside.
 Instead, you try to give
those drawings to a child
and I am convinced
that he will continue.
Not only time,but age
also has the power
to take away our superpowers,

it steals our dreams,
turning a rainbow into
a silly grey cloud.

THANKS

Wherever you turn, you see it
between the irises
of others and the lips
of strangers.
You can hear it
in the chirping of birds,
in the strong wind,stretched
through your hair.
It reaches your eyes
and makes its way into your heart,
it is the light
that I follow, wherever it goes.
It guides me through life
and through the thousand seasons.
The heart that still sings,
the soul that still jumps higher...
I'll hold her by the hand,
because she is strength.
Because I am a man
and one day, I will disappear.
I have a dream to fulfill,
but I don't know by what time or date.
But with a smile and strength,
even the greatest failure
will seem like an attraction
on the merry-go-round.

MISSING

I was navigating inside
my thought,
losing myself in the thick fog.
I didn't take my eyes off the horizon,
which seemed as deep
and boundless,as the many silences
that have been echoing for centuries,
like screams inside my soul.
I remember the beautiful,
sweet, happy moments,
luminescent as stars
in the present, perennial night,
that envelops the head.
And I fight on the front
against enemies,
more skilled than myself,
but with the fire,that from
so many sides,differentiates the soul,
I do not surrender...
I advance beyond the "memento"
I have about her.
I lower my eyes to the sea
and see my face,
gloomy and disconsolate,
submerged in the surreal landscape,
but in which I didn't stand out.
Step by step, I was giving up,

but a gust of hope lifted me up.
After all, he,who is born
a rock,ends in gravel.

THE LIGHT

And I close my eyes,
like bar shutters after closing time.
The silence falls gloomily,
capping in my throat
every scream of white hope.
On my sanguine lips,hangs
the slow word,
imbued with a strong meaning of love.
The sky, light-blue coloured
is mirrored in my bright iris,
wet with emotion,
inflated by a massive dose of desire,
to amaze the hearts of others.
After dark periods
in the grip of loneliness,
now,with you,maiden,
I share hope and future,
to realise the present,
by rewriting our lives, page after page.
Let us reseed the beautiful vineyard,
to drink in the future a good wine,
worthy of our fine palates.

ONE DOLLAR POEM

It mirrors itself and enchants,
without ever taking her eyes off the iris.
A tear descends swiftly from the step,
which seems as transparent as her soul.
She grips her hands tightly,
as if trying to break the chains
that bind her and do not let
her live freely,away from her fears.
Her eyes are easy prey for the light,
a fresh breeze of wind caresses her hair,
it flies away accompanied
by the warm rustle of a sentiment,
now stale and worn out by time.
He clasps his hands together,
clasps the hope of a better tomorrow.
It will be like a phoenix,
From its ashes, it will rise again:
young, strong and full of life,
it will be like a spark, still lit from a fire,
which, at first glance, seems extinguished,
but instead,waits for that thread
of wind to return to burning.
When you fail,
you have the opportunity
to start from scratch...
And from nothing,you build an empire.

ROSE OF WINDS

I stare at the ceiling,
contemplating the ticking rain.
All is beautifully silent
I smile at the glow
of some lightning,
which, unconsciously,
illuminates my thoughts.
My eyes open, but in reality,
they are closed.
They reflect the soul,
kissing slowly,
little by little,
the idea of success.
Happy and alive is the thought
I have the absolute desire
for some real caress,
kiss or an original embrace,
that would cancel the evil
of the past,
which, until today,
has only fed me
with false things.

YOU JUST HAVE TO BELIEVE IT

The memory still burns solemnly
inside my eyes.
 The wind is strong,
swiftly trying to sweep
away the grey clouds,
which in the early evening
bathed the earth.
It takes even bad weather,
to make the flowers bloom.
It takes defeat,to make
us even hungrier,
 to make us determined to fight
for another victory.
Believing in ourselves is the key
to any success, believing in us
is the medicine to make us happy.
The surrounding nature smiles,
watered by the torrential rain.
Now,it grows strong in the sunlight.
Let the pain of the past
form the strength of your future.
Let memory condition the present,
to make it sweet and strong,
under the meaning of the verb "redeem".

STRADIVARI SQUARE*

Silence populates the streets
of this eternal city.
The hiss of the wind is heard
among the brick buildings,.
And us?
We were talking under the plants, while
a few leaves, slowly, settled
on the road surface.
Among the shrubs of the center
and the rustle of the water,
gushing from the fountain
under the tower, something dense
was peeping out in the darkness.
Now, only the memory accompanies us,
a dense memory,
which, like a fog when it descends,
blurs our vision,
erasing everything that comes into view.
How can we forget your hands?
I held them for years within
the walls of our city.
I have a dense memory
of love even today.
As I write these sentences,
we may be sunset, but Cremona...
Cremona, remember,
is beautiful, even at night.

** Poem dedicated to Cremona*

THE ORCHESTRA

The song of the crickets
continued after the night.
A light breeze of wind
swept away the remaining clouds,
that, before the birth of the day,
obscured my gaze.
The same clouds,
which are now tinged
with a thousand colours at dawn.
In the distance, light flashes
of lightning can still be seen,
brass-coloured flashes,followed
by some timid thunder,
as a reminder of the power
of the storm, now past.
The gentle day enjoys
a warm temperature,
thus,helping the awakening
from the restless night.
Among the harvest,
I hear only my own thoughts,
accompanied like an orchestra,
with sounds belonging to nature.
Slowly, the sun sets,
causing again the wandering of the night.

FRATER (Brother)

The wind knocks
at the window
The thunder calls
with a powerful voice
It's raining,
the drops are racing
on the glass,
as we did as children,
with our bicycles in the street.
You-arm,
I shoulder or vice versa,
commanded by a single brain,
whose brotherly thought is equality.
It's raining, on this Saturday night,
now,never sad,
finished, like the last drink we shared.
We have been through a lot,
but we have overcome
many with a smile:
from the most bitter cold
to the hottest summer,
from seeing the flowers blooming
to seeing the leaves falling.
Many have left us,
many have been the protagonists,
but only we have remained
in our eternal lives,

we, who consider ourselves
belonging to the same blood.
There is no truer love than friendship
There is no more beautiful place,
in which to shelter from the storm.
It's raining, brother,
shall we go out?

IT'S SO ROTTEN

The smile on your face appears,
erasing every flaw.
The moment gives way to time,
anger gives way to affection.
Time flows, like water from a torrent
We are poor fish, at the mercy of the current.
The world turns, but does not change
There are people who hate each
other and kill each other.
A drop falls from the sky, like a tear
So many men are so greedy,
that they have forgotten they have a soul.
We're all on the same level,
from those who work in a factory,
to those who earn money on the couch.
No human life has a price.

THE MOON CALLS

I stare at the sky,
 the thought is calm.
Slowly, it flies away.

The sea sings,
under the dark sky,
strong words.

It leaves silences,
interrupted by the wind
that cuddles me.

I hear your words
closing my eyes,
sitting alone.

The moon shines
like a spark,
shining quietly.

Sweet summer,
you, who reign supreme,
warm the heart.

DEPTH

The waves break
in the silence,
the lights
of the lighthouses
alternate like the fluttering
of eyelashes.
Stars like eyes stare
at you and enchant you.
A light breeze of wind
caresses your face,
as if there were the gentle hands
of a mother.
For hours,
I hear the voice of the sea,
which speaks to my unconscious
in a suffocating way.
Memories emerge
from my depths,
like old wrecks that have gone,
unnoticed for years.
Sometimes,
I cry to feel stronger
In those tears,
I shed all my suffering,
to free my soul from the chains.

THE SNAKE AND THE PHOENIX

I don't know what is more painful:
 losing yourself or not seeing
happiness any more.
It attacks you and blinds you
It takes away every crutch of rebellion,
at every attempt of conquest.
Inside you, it tries to create its lair,
it ruins your memories,
it steals years of your life,
it makes you feel inferior to everyone,
in order to manipulate you.
Take refuge in the smiles
of others and react!
Remember that all great things
have always been in history
preceded by nothing.
You all have the chance to react,
starting again from the rubble.
Life goes on, despite
the seriousness of the events.
Step by step, the path will change,
it may become more tortuous,
but more enlightened.
Slowly, you will no longer be solo violins,
but part of a splendid orchestra.
Be like the ones called Phoenix,
that, despite the gruesome death,

rise majestically from their ashes.
Let negativity crawl alone in the tall grass.

AUGUST

The rising sun
People chatting on the shoreline
Me walking along the sea,
thinking, dreaming,
but above all,fighting daily battles,
for which dying would worth it.
The day passes quickly,
like the emotions felt
during the day's arc.
We are little misunderstood artists,
but determined to bring
our ideal to the top.
Evening falls and under the sunset,
with my beer, I contemplate
the years passed in suffering.
The night falls gracefully and I,
thief of dreams,
 gaze at the heavenly vault,
never so bright.
I lie on a sunbed,
alone with the sea,
narrating with its voice.
The wind is cradling me,
the stars are pointing
the sailors' way,
for returning home.

My thoughts were lost
in the deafening silence,
while my soul went out the door,
to rest in total serenity.

ETERNAL*

In my thoughts,
I lose myself,
sweet is the memory
of his gaze.
The walks in the center,
in front of the tower,
made you brighter.
Lush is your voice,
as strong as your perfume,
that years later,
still pervades my mind.
Your lips,like a home for my soul,
 Your hands,
as warm
as summer on the plain.
Your green eyes,
like the hope
that never dies.
You will shine again,
you will heal my wounds
and blows,
because Cremona
is beautiful, even at night.
It sings of nature,
it is surrounded by culture.
The violin plays,
as sweet as your voice

It moves me like the first "ti amo",
whispered almost playfully,
before the spectacle
of our Romanesque city.
So many lights that together
teach us how great you are.
You alone are great.

*Poem dedicated to Cremona; read on the occasion
of the event "Poetic Attack in the Square"*

HAPPINESS

What is happiness?
Well, there's no answer to that.
There isn't one because
happiness cannot be summed up
in a simple definition.
Happiness hides,
it often fools us by deceiving us,
but it never abandons us.
Where is she? Where is she?
Why does it hides from our touch?
It does so,out of fear
of being synthesised
into something abstract,
as man has done for billions of years.
Happiness is everywhere,
look for it!
Don't give up! It's there,
it doesn't forget us.
And if, at times,
it seems to tease us,
it's because it wants
to be cradled, just like a child.
Smile today, before time turns
everything into a memory
and from memory into remorse.
Love,love more than ever!
Sow positivity

and let the occasional storm come,
because thanks to it,
you will grow
and be nourished
and become lush.
Remember that winter
is also needed
for a warm and gentle summer.
Man is distinguished from animals
by his consciousness and intellect.
Every day, every day...
 we must raise the bar
and aim higher,
because we can only grow.
Dream to achieve,
don't just dream!
Life is a choice and we must
choose to live,
not to exist.
Let's make this one life
of ours precious,
precious not only for ourselves,
but for those
we love and care about.

MAGRITTE

The emptiness inside me
wears me down,
more than the beatings
I have suffered.
Words hurt more than hands.
A tear falls quickly,
that slowly cuts my cheek in half.
I remember his soft hands,
that first caressed my face.
The whispered "I love you",
followed by intense kisses,
our perfect love,
persuasive to the perception
of my eye,
blinded by the heart.
Time has consumed us
and changed us,
our love like a "magritte".
Every evening is a kiss
on my angels' foreheads,
because love may cease
to be in a couple,
but it will never cease
between mother and children.
I protect them from brutality,
I want the world to apologise
to them tomorrow.

I pretend everything is fine,
but I cry every night.
I try to dream
He has chained me,
taking away my freedom
I can no longer fly
Life is not pain and falsehood
I don't believe it,
I don't want to believe it.
Love is not evil, I trust in it,
I know that it will return
and it will not kill me.

THE ART OF LIVING

Everyone applauded, all, except one person.Like little soldiers, silent and attentive throughout the show, and at the end, a triumph of applause.

The grey tormented the black, creating shades that, however deep, did not give a glimmer of light,but only relief to the shadows.

Among the audience, those two eyes stared at me, as blue as the sea,because you could have drown in them.Among the whole audience, I was looking for her clapping hands.

I wanted to amaze her, or rather, to surprise her. I took a red balloon and tied it to the branch of a plant, leaving it to the wind.

The audience didn't understand well,they were noisy. They are adults,they don't see beyond things. They were railing against my change of programme, but those blue eyes didn't get upset, they stayed there, staring at my show, so I took some colours, a canvas and threw these colours on it: yellow like the sun and happiness, green like hope, blue like the night with its stars...

They looked so beautiful and hypnotic,in contrast with black and white. Everyone was booing and criticising, but she was applauding and, you know, I consider that my greatest success. I took the microphone and said: "Ladies and gentlemen, the art of living".

The night was falling, but even darkness with the right frame has its charm. Try to be yourselves in the eyes

of those who really appreciate you and distinguish
yourselves from monotony,because it is harmful to us
and to our art.

AT THE EDGES

After the performance, I hurried to the dressing room.
I changed and went out to talk to her, but I didn't see
her. I looked for her in the hall, among the people who
were pushing me and mocking me for the figure I had
made on stage.My shirt was stained with paint, but I
didn't care.
I just wanted to talk to her...
I didn't find her.
In the days when there were following the theatre re-
hearsals, everyone avoided me, so I decided to quit,
even though acting was more than just a job to me.
I stayed at home alone and thought about those blue
eyes all the time, so deep and dense.Just thinking
about them confused me inside and created a mess.
I wanted to react to this darkness, by trying to make
the most of that small glimmer of light,seen in that iris,
so I took my first pair of shoes and went out.
I went in front of the tree,where I used to go when I
was a child,and I stared at it. Inside, I travelled a thou-
sand miles.The important thing was not to get lost in
the maze of the psyche,
because the psyche is harmful, when everything outsi-
de is colourless.
As I stared at that plant,I felt like a child again
 and slowly,I felt an immense relief of love.
Silently and swiftly from behind, she came from who
knows where, she shook my hand in front of the tree

and I felt happy, out of danger.I no longer felt like a small ship in the middle of the sea, but now in the darkness, I felt like a great star. When you lose your way, you must not forget happiness, it is there.... It can be found in the eyes of other people, in small gestures, in successes, but do you think it can even be found in suffering?Happiness must be cared for and cradled like a child. We are all travellers in search of ourselves, in order to find a shred of truth. In the midst of so much falsehood,we push not only our own boundaries, but even beyond them, to discover unknown parts of our soul. Do not be afraid to stray beyond your boundaries, dare ... Dream today, to come true tomorrow! Cry today,to smile stronger tomorrow!

THE ART OF SILENCE

I returned home, now,
the sun had never set
My mind was lost in the mist,
like a ship in the sea,
slowly disappearing
over the horizon.
I opened the front door
and sat down on the sofa
I turned off all the lights,
because I wanted darkness
I wanted to lose myself again,
in my silence.
I felt her hands on my shoulders again,
warm and gentle,
against my wounded
and alone soul.
That darkness became
light in my eyes,
my silence slowly took on a voice.
Her hands, the same ones
that had been clapping
that night, were on the back
of my neck, caressing me,
ready to protect me in the future.
She bent down,
she whispered a phrase,
that still tortures me in my thoughts:

"Ladies and gentlemen,
the art of living".
She said it smiling
and while she was saying it,
she clasped my hand
with her other hand.
She didn't stop talking there,
she added:
"You chose colours because
it is only with colours,
That one chooses to live
and not to exist".
I didn't understand
and asked her what she meant,
but she didn't answer.
She wanted me to find
the answers in my silence,
a particularly noisy
and chatty silence,
which was taking more
and more part inside me.
Slowly, those hands vanished
I no longer felt them,
but at the same time,
I felt warmth in my chest,
I fell asleep happy,
confused, but happy.
The next morning,
I took the car keys

and decided to go to the sea,
where I often went as a child.
I wanted to feel again
the same sensation
that I felt in front of the oak tree.
I went in front of the lighthouse,
amidst the silence of nature
and the stillness of the wind
I sat on a rock and meditated,
but I felt nothing,
I felt no presence and no sensation,
until a gentle voice reminded me,
that only in my silence,
I could find the answers.
Don't look for the answers
inside other people
They will never have the same answers
that you could find within yourself.
Love to love, don't just love!

CALAMAIO
(Ink pot)

I stare at the ceiling and my gaze is lost in the dark-
ness,surrounding my face
My open eyes seem closed
Your voice echoes, like the uncontested ticking of time.
An unaccustomed,but tasty memory of defeat in my
eyes takes center stage
You were smiling beside me and I had my heart in my
hand.
The rain that rumbles outside whispers a lullaby, as if
trying to snatch me from the darkness of my uncon-
scious
A loud and overbearing thunder,similar to our first
quarrel,frightens me, increasing my heartbeat
I loved you like a mother and esteemed you like a father.
Persuasive, your gaze always brought me to my knees,
bending me in a cry, as long as the night,and then,cul-
minating in the gentle, spring-like peace of your arms,
the same arms that time and life have taken away from
me, separated like rails, hat will never meet again.
Parallel lines, but forever intangible.
In the most beautiful mistakes and in the strongest me-
mories, I will visit you forever.

NUCLEAR SUNSETS

All is beautifully silent
Only the uncontested whistling
of the wind is heard.
The last cricket sings solemnly,
as if anticipating the imminent cold.
My eye rests on the blades
of grass which, like waves,
move before my figure.
My steps, as fast as
the clouds in the sky,
follow one another
in an uncontrolled advance,
paraphonable to time
and by time, to life itself.
Like a predator,
loneliness stalks my figure
a strange sensation of fragility.
The impending winter descends,
like night on a cool sunny day.
There is no room for emotion
in a colourless world,
incapable of recognising
three-dimensional figures,
giving equal value
and depth to things.

CURRENT WATER

I wonder if tomorrow
you will be by my side,
smiling and happy,
with deep,
almost shining eyes,
like a sunbeam
reflected in the mirror.
I wonder if it will be you,
holding my arm
White and wise soul,
protector of my fragile heart,
like origami.
I wonder how time can dare
to age such beauty
I would like to immortalise
you on a sheet of paper,
to preserve you
from such a destiny,
from which you deserve
a way out.
I wonder if you 'll say
goodnight to me,
even though I'm already asleep.
Will you be there?
Who knows if time will grant
us such a privilege?
All we can do is wait

for the days to ripen,
letting time to flow inexorably,
like water from a stream.

RUPOPHOBIA

Pay no attention to the past step!
Do not turn to look
at the already taken path!
Keep your eyes fixed
on a distinct point before you.
The past will always hurt,
but in the world of memories,
a wound heals in time,
becoming a scar.
Set yourself dreams,
but don't get lost in them.
They exist to be fulfilled.
Dream, dare, fight! Only thus,
life can be lived.
Life must be won,
otherwise, you will remain stuck
in the concept of physical existence.
Love yourself, before you make
yourself loved!
Do not make yourself
an idol or a hero!
In the world,there is not
the most heavenly perfection.

CARESSES OF MEMORIES

I hear delicate notes
coming from a piano
My mind, at once,
playfully throws
our last smoothie in my face
The smiles, the torn kisses between
one step and the next,
the hands that clasped strong,
cohesive, in the hope of resisting
in the present and the future.
The lost gaze rests,
light as a feather,
delicate because
of fear, on a dusty photo,
left there to fade with time.
I, who still have your perfume
imprinted in my memory,
how can I expect to lose you in my heart?
I, who still remember
your caresses,
how can I claim to hate you?
Those eyes...
so angelic and hypnotic,
that still enrapture my dreams,
making them vain
to the suffering of the future.
How can I forget them?

MARRIAGE

It murmurs angrily
and menacingly
the foamy, strong
and frightened sea.
The wind blows undisturbed,
tousling my hair,
whistling through the sails
that have landed
and are firmly in the harbour.
It swells the waves of the sea,
as if to provoke them
Decorous tints of foam arise,
swelling and tossing in the surf,
tearing the stillness and the silence,
giving voice to their grit,
painted, as a whole.
I sit and stare at the immensity
of the horizon before me
so boundless.
I appear so tiny in its presence,
coloured with celestial shades,
alternating with greyish clouds,
that with their bulk,
are reflected in the sea.
I sit and wait for the sun
to go down
slowly, little by little,

some star, so far away,
but never so...

SWALLOWS OUT OF SEASON

Torrid heat in the middle
of winter
I tie my jumper around
my waist
and keep my T-shirt on.
The thoughts that alternate like
the seasons are many.
A constant confusion,
daughter of a sentiment
which has become stale,
destined to a profound stylisation
of events,
more and more serious
and terrifying.
Butterflies dancing
over primroses,
blossomed out of season
Pre-ripe as an over-hasty declaration
of love.
Precious as if it were
the last breath.
Every day, we stare at the sky
and marvel at the immensity
of the cosmos, we lose sight
of the stars and planets,
marvelling at the distance
we are from it.

We no longer appreciate
what we have
We want more and more
and end up losing everything.
A swallow flies,
heralding the imminent arrival
of spring.
Dancing, a shy butterfly
like the meow
of a newborn cat,
delicate as a mother's caress
to her child.
Admirable balances
of a unique ecosystem
Co-tenants of the same planet,
that it would be better
to remember to call home.

PARALLELS

Silences
boundless silences
before me present
themselves now
like a wall of fog
I do not see any silhouette
before my path,
empty and alone.
Surrounded by the creaking
of a few branches,
trampled by my step,
I advance determined,
but not caring
about my direction,
wandering thoughtfully,
without a destination.
Broken in half
Devoid of hope in solitude
I stand, like a river flowing
into the sea.
I no longer understand anything,
except your absence,
so light to others' eyes,
but so overbearing
and harsh to my touch.
On the other hand,
we are parallels

so similar geometrically speaking,
but so far from each other,
destined to never touch.
Yet, from some perspective,
deceiving the eye,
we are born
from the same point.
We can only chase each
other endlessly,
without ever meeting.

FELLING A CENTURIES-OLD OAK TREE

Bowed head,gaze fixed on my shoes,while the drops of rain fall from my hood, as they do from a gutter. All is silent, all remains beatifully, to listen to my whim, son of an unnatural selfishness,dictated by the past.
Ever more painfully, the loneliness from within devours me, slowly, one piece at a time, it remains invisible to the eyes of those who are closest to me.
The tears mingle with the rain
The swollen eyes give a way only to the heartbreaking sobbing of my body
I miss a hug,
I miss a caress... Every day, we have the task to amaze. But amaze who? Who else, but ourselves! I give in one step at a time, one brick at a time and I bare myself, like plants in autumn, leaving the eye a landscape of depression and desolation.
I sit and think... I sit and I want to change, I sit and I surrender, I sit and I cry.... More and more... The fog erases my figure, as lightly as a veil, making me part of the surrounding landscape, like the trees and dry branches, left to rot on the edges of the canals.
I die inside, poisoned by memories, I die inside,poisoned by parts of me that I thought to be allies, by parts of me that I thought to be essential to my life.
I die inside from a failed coexistence between idealism and pride.

DESOLATION OF A WANDERING THINKER

Every step I take,
the silence interrupts,
the moon peeks through
the leaves and shyly,
lights my way.
My thought is lost on the horizon,
in this impervious path.
I rest like a leaf
on the ground
I fall dancing to the wind,
as much as to the emotions
felt in life a continuous
overflow of feelings,
blossoming under a fresh,
spring sun.
I think of you immersed
in the most intimate silence,
interrupted only by the chirping
of a few birds,
passing over my head
and the uncontested rustling
of the wind,
which, like a hand,
gently pampers
the surrounding shrubs.
More and more lost,
among the paths

of my unconscious,
I rediscover old tendernesses,
shelved like boxes
in my memory.
My conscience murmurs
with a continuous ringing voice,
like the continuous gushing
of waters from a spring.
Its pain is caused by your loss,
underlined by a swarm
of memories and emotions,
sharp as razors for my soul.
The moon almost tiptoes down,
leaving room
for the theatrical birth
of the sun, hiding fears
and sorrows,
illuminating faces,
correcting hearts.

A YOUNG, DISCONSOLATE PIANIST

The night, like a blanket,
envelops me,
a trickle of air gently
caresses my hair,
and everything around me
is beautifully silent.
Heartbreaking silences,
like biting screams,
are inside my deepest self.
A light in front of me,
cold as winter,
attracts my gaze like a magnet
Before it, so small,
I do appear:a wretched man.
The black,r eflecting waters
of the celestial vault numb
the surrounding landscape.
I sit and gaze at the desolation
and eternal inexplicability of things,
alone and helpless,
I think and rethink
of my worldly life:
To the not given goodbyes,
To the hands that were
never held tightly enough,
To the love you never said,
but only breathed,

To the hearts I broke
and only made them suffer,
To my arms, too fragile
to protect anyone,
to you... who will mourn
my absence,more than anyone else.
I will be there, ike the North Star,
one light among many,
but the only one to point
you in the right direction.

XV APRIL GALLERY

A thought arises,
at the tolling of the hand
A strong feeling
of abandonment envelops me
like a blanket,
at the stroke of midnight.
The surrounding darkness
highlights the blood,
spilt by the painful cuts,
incised on my heart.
I wait in vain for your message,
to appease the untameable
sovereign force of lack,
a daughter, lack of all those attentions
we gave each other:
How are you?
What are you doing?
Did you smile?
What did you eat?
Finished work?
How did it go?
All those attentions
were often summed up in a hug,
so strong and dense,
that it frequently brought
my shyness to its knees.
You and I,

wind and sea,
moon and tide.
You and I,
so far away from each other,
but still today,
after years,
we condition ourselves.
You and I,
destined to follow each other,
like rails,
that parallel to each other will
never touch,
but from different perspectives,
they will seem closer and closer,
until they touch.

ON TIPTOE

I wonder if I appear happy
in the eyes of others
Who knows if in the dawn,
I stand out, like a half moon.
I walk slowly through
the blades of grass,
I lose my identity
in the multitude
of thoughts, captured
by my attention,
as a spider's web does
with insects.
In my eyes, in addition
to the colour of the iris,
a tangle of reflective ideas
of the surreal mess appears,
almost glacial, present inside me.
Lightly dancing like a snowflake,
a yellowish leaf, victim of the cold,
blown by the wind to the ground,
rests, as time does with the emotions
inside us, the more time passes
and the more the weather strikes them,
causing them to swell, until they wither.
Besides, all plants need water,
But too much... rots them.

DESOLATION OF A BRIGAND

You,
who do not respect
any living being,
You,
who have no problem
finding food or drinking water,
You,
who do not respect
any different way
of thinking, think...
Think if it is really worth it
to exist with this guilty conscience,
stained by hatred,
blinded by who knows what.
You,
who work serenely, think,
think if it is really worth it.
There are those who have nothing
and have turned nothing into wealth.
You,
who say you love, teach me!
I will make a gift of it.
You,
who say you have a true laugh,
discern for me falsehood.
You,
who consider yourself poor,

teach me to be as poor as thyself,
for I have nothing left,but to weep.
My hands are cut off,
my eyes blinded by sweat,
pain is nothing but a soundtrack,
unheard in a film, now unseen,
but by the wrong eye.
The world, in spite
of everything, will not stop
waiting for me
and it will continue to turn in error.
Don't ignore my cry, brother
because there will be no forgiveness
for your silence.
Hold out your hand and help me!
You,
who consider yourself poor,
teach me to be poor like you.

www.ingramcontent.com/pod-product-compliance
Lightning Source LLC
Chambersburg PA
CBHW031351160726
47993CB00002B/913